The Love and Power Journal

Also by Lynn Andrews

BOOKS
LOVE AND POWER

The Medicine Woman Series:
MEDICINE WOMAN
FLIGHT OF THE SEVENTH MOON
JAGUAR WOMAN
STAR WOMAN
CRYSTAL WOMAN: The Sisters of the Dreamtime
WINDHORSE WOMAN: A Marriage of Spirit
WOMAN OF WYRRD:
The Arousal of the Inner Fire
SHAKKAI: Woman of the Sacred Garden
WOMAN AT THE EDGE OF TWO WORLDS:
The Spiritual Journey Through Menopause
DARK SISTER: A Sorcerer's Love Story

AUDIOCASSETTES
UP THE MOUNTAIN
POWER ANIMAL IN THE MASK
PARENT TREE BOOK OF THE CHILD
ACT OF POWER
IMAGINATION
LUMINOUS FIBERS
EARTH WISDOM • DEATH AND TRANSITION

AUDIOCASSETTES (cont'd)
SACRED DREAMS AND PAST LIVES
KEEPER OF THE BRAIN
WHITE STAR WOMAN
SPIRIT RETRIEVAL
CRYSTAL DOMAIN OF THE SACRED MASTERS
CENTERING MEDITATION
PRACTICAL WISDOM I & II
JOURNEY INTO THE DREAMTIME
ENTERING THE POWER DECK
THE MASK OF POWER TAPE SET
WOMAN AT THE EDGE OF TWO WORLDS TAPE SET
THE GATHERINGS AT JOSHUA TREE TAPE SETS

WORKBOOKS AND CARDS
TEACHINGS AROUND THE SACRED WHEEL
*THE POWER DECK: THE CARDS OF WISDOM
*THE MASK OF POWER
WALK IN BALANCE:
Meditations with Lynn Andrews
WALK IN SPIRIT: Prayers for the Seasons of Life
*WOMAN AT THE EDGE OF TWO WORLDS:
Menopause and the Feminine Rites of Passage

*Has companion audiocassette(s)

All of the above are available at your local bookstore.

ⓟ   ⓟ   ⓟ

Please visit the Hay House Website at: **www.hayhouse.com**

The Love and Power Journal

A Workbook for the Fine Art of Living

Lynn V. Andrews

Hay House, Inc.
Carlsbad, California • Sydney, Australia

Published and distributed in the United States by:
Hay House, Inc., P.O. Box 5100, Carlsbad, CA 92018-5100
(800) 654-5126 • (800) 650-5115 (fax)

Edited by: Charel Morris and Jill Kramer   *Designed by:* Delia Frees and Wendy Lutge

ISBN 1-56170-849-6

04 03 02 01   5 4 3 2
1st printing, February 1999
2nd printing, August 2001

Printed in China through Palace Press International

This book is lovingly dedicated to you, the reader, for your courage and willingness to explore the wilderness of your own soul.

Creating Your Own Sacred Circle

Spiritual work is often singular work, done in private. I know you may have traveled your sacred path alone up to this point. Yet many of you have asked me how you can find your own sacred circle—a few spiritual friends to work with and to grow with on a regular basis. Consider using this journal as a starting point to begin your work with others. Invite some friends to gather weekly, and begin journeying together. As you move through each week in this journal, celebrate your discoveries and share your insights with each other. If it is time for you to work with others, contact me for more information about creating a sacred circle.

Contents

Acknowledgments

I would like to thank all of the apprentices in my school of Sacred Arts and Training for providing such wonderful mirrors in my own process of learning. They have been, and continue to be, an inspiration and an invaluable resource in teaching me about the balance between love and power.

I would also like to thank Charel Morris and Delia Frees for their continued support of my work. Thank you for your tireless efforts on this book and in all of my work.

Introduction

There came a time in my personal journey when I knew I wanted to work with a woman teacher, and while many of my friends were being drawn to various Eastern spiritual practices, I was being called in another direction. My path was leading me to work with, and to understand, the wisdom of the West. For more than a decade I have shared my journey with you, and I have shared the wisdom of my teachers, Agnes Whistling Elk, Ruby Plenty Chiefs, and the other amazing women of the Sisterhood of the Shields. As many of you know, I never planned on becoming a "seer," as Agnes calls me. But it is the journey that the Great Spirit presented to me, and I have never regretted my decision to step on to this path of heart. I can hear Agnes saying to me, "We are all called to a sacred journey, but it is our choice as to whether or not we answer."

My journey has presented me with many gifts and surprises. I never thought that I would become a teacher or create a school of sacred arts, but that is exactly what I have done. As I became full with the beauty and the power of the teachings I was receiving, it became clear to me that I had little choice but to share the knowledge that had been imparted to me. It was as though I had found an abundant source of food and water, and I knew there were, and still are, many who hunger for this healing food, who thirst for this sacred water. For the past 15 years, I have moved out into the world, working with literally thousands of people through my words, at the various gatherings I hold, and through our School of Sacred Arts and Training.

As a seer, I have worked with a wide range of people, and the work is different with each one. I have approached this workbook with that concept in mind, and have created a journey within these pages that will allow you to discover your own path. The book is designed to cover a year of linear time, but if you wish, you can move more quickly or more slowly. However, if you *are* moving more slowly, look at whether your need for perfection is what is slowing you down. Perfection is an addiction that will keep you from your own enlightenment. I want you to be impeccable in your work, but that does not mean *perfect*. Do the best you can and be honest with yourself, but there is no perfection within this book, just as there is no perfection within life—except, of course, to say that everything is perfect just the way it is.

If you are moving more quickly through this workbook, ask yourself whether you are exploring the weekly reflection and contemplations as deeply as you can. Do you find yourself rushing through life, not pausing to enjoy the magic of a small moment in time? Regardless of the time you take to complete these teachings, it is very important to do the work in the order in which it is presented. If you wish, you can go back to a section and repeat the work, knowing that each time you approach a particular teaching, you will learn something new. But please don't jump ahead. Do your best, but do the work and keep moving forward. Find your own rhythm within these pages, and then move with the energy.

We are all unique, needing different challenges to grow. Each week I will ask you to do various types of inner work. It is essential for us each to create a strong foundation of physical, emotional, spiritual, and mental health and well-being. We will start by first balancing these four areas. I will then ask you to explore more advanced work and various techniques that will bring you into the realm of higher consciousness. Each one of you will have your own experiences to work with and to learn from. Together we will develop intent, we will work with the power of the sacred wheel, and we will learn how energy flows and how this flow of energy within us and around us can affect our relationships, our creativity, and our health.

I am a shaman, a teacher and a healer. That is who I am in the world. Shamanism, or the art of seeing, is the ability to relate to the forces of the natural world; it is a path to power and mastery. In our Western culture, we are very connected by language, by words. Just as words bring us together, they can also begin to bind us to a reality, a point of view, that no longer holds true for us. Words are a sacred tool and must be honored as such. When used carefully, words have magical healing properties. When used to judge, to hate, or to separate, words are deadly. The words you will be using in this workbook are your basic tools for healing on this journey. Treat them with respect. Honor your words.

As we evolve and connect with the ancient soul within us, we face the challenge of finding a new means of expression, creating a new language—possibly a new set of symbols to express whom we have become. This work that we are doing together will have a profound and healing effect on the world around us. I welcome you with open arms as you step on to your own path of heart. It is my honor and my privilege to share in this part of your journey. As my teachers would probably remind me, tasks are so much easier when done with good friends. Welcome to our journey of finding love and power and the gateways into the mystery.

— Lynn V. Andrews, Summer 1998

How to Approach This Book

I n my book *Love and Power*, I italicized certain sentences to indicate that these were ideas that had been of special help to me in my life—teachings that had, perhaps, changed my life forever. This workbook will assist you in exploring many of these teachings, providing you with a foundation for balancing love and power in your own life. In the back of your workbook are Personal Pages for you to write down your thoughts and record the truths you discover on your journey. Moving thoughts and ideas out of your head and onto a written page is one of the best tools of self-discovery I know of.

Most weeks, you will be presented with a concept, an idea, or a point of view to reflect on. Read this *Reflection* each day of that particular week. These *Reflections* are truths that need your attention. Meditate on them. Read them out loud. Let the words dance through your mind, knowing that language has rhythm and creates form. Allow them to move through you over and over. Some will flow through you like a gentle stream, while others may tumble and collide like water cascading over a waterfall. Notice how these words feel in your *bodymind*. Use your imagination to see if you can taste or smell the idea. This may seem foreign to you at first, but play with it.

I have also provided you with many *Ideas to Contemplate*. These consist of questions to ponder, ideas to consider, and work to do. As the *Reflections* and the *Ideas to*

Contemplate begin to stir up your own energy, spend time journaling in the Personal Pages. When you make a discovery for yourself or have a realization, use these special pages to create a document of your truths and insights.

Some weeks I will give you a **Sacred Practice** to do. I may ask you to do the same **Sacred Practice** several months later so that you can be aware of your movement and growth. Many people tell me of their frustrations, thinking they have not accomplished anything in their life so far. In our Western culture, we are so goal oriented that before we complete one goal, we have usually set three more for ourselves. We barrel through the successful completion of a goal with our eyes firmly fixed on the next goal. We never acknowledge ourselves for what we have accomplished in the moment, for the goals we have reached. We end up feeling as though we have let ourselves and everyone else down, when the truth is that we have done what we set out to do. Goals are wonderful. Understand that having goals is not the problem. The problem is that we don't allow ourselves to live in the moment, to notice what is changing and evolving within us every day, every minute. If you are always focused on the future, chasing down the next goal, you will miss the magic and the mystery of life. It is in the mystery that you will discover love and power.

The Sacred Wheel

When working with someone, I use the sacred wheel as a paradigm for the process of mind. It is especially helpful when working with abstract concepts. If we take a simple wheel and divide it like a compass into four directions, we have physicalness and manifestation in the south, transformation and emotions in the west, spirit in the north, and mind in the east. When we use the paradigm of the wheel, we learn to look at life from a circular perspective, to see the wholeness of life. With certain teachings in this workbook, I ask you to move around the wheel, looking at the four directions. Each direction provides you with mirrors that have a particular reflection because of what that direction relates to. The concept of the Sacred Wheel will make more sense when you actually begin to use it.

Let's work together now on the "Power Statement": *For power to be present in your life, you must make a place inside you for power to live.* Now I want you to write the "Power Statement" in the center of the wheel.

Now move to the SOUTH, or bottom quadrant of your circle. Always begin in the south, because it represents the physical world, the world of manifestation. It is also the home of the child. In the south, look at how this idea relates to your childhood, to your inner child, and to your physical environment. How do you approach this thought from the way you experience your physical life, from where power lives physically within you? How does your environment reflect the concept of *being a place for power to live?* Do you feel powerful when you are in your environment? Does this concept relate to your childhood? Sometimes looking back at your own childhood will provide

The Sacred Wheel

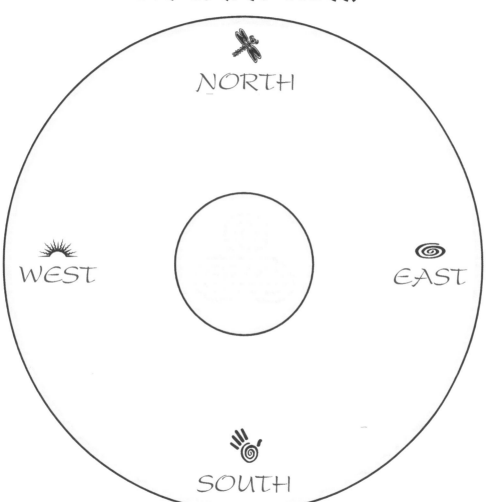

NORTH

WEST

EAST

SOUTH

7

a strong reflection. Just ask yourself the questions, and then listen for your answers. Write your insights in the south of the wheel.

The WEST, or left quadrant of your circle, is the place of emotion. It is also the home of the adolescent, the teenager experiencing first love and trying to figure out where he or she fits in the world. It is in the west that you will find mirrors of trans-formation, mirrors of death and rebirth. It is in the west that you may find shadows and the darkness that will define the light within you. Once again, look at the "Power Statement," but this time look at the reflection of the west mirror. Approach it from the emotional part of yourself, asking how you feel about power, if you allow power inside you, or if you are afraid of it—afraid of what it means to take your power. Ask your-self when it is that you become an emotional adolescent. Do you lose power when you react more like a rebellious teenager than a passionate adult? Now, once again, write your insights in the west of the wheel.

NORTH, or the upper quadrant of your circle, is the place of spirit. It reflects your relationship to God, the Goddess, or the Great Spirit. North represents the adult, a responsible, independent, balanced being. We find inspiration in the north. Face the north, your spiritual essence, and look at the "Power Statement," exploring how you feel about power from a spiritual perspective. Do you feel that only God deserves power and you do not? Do you think that spiritual people are weak or timid, that being spiritual means letting the events of the world just happen to you? Do you trust your adult self to be powerful? Are you willing to accept the responsibility of being a pow-erful adult? Do these questions bring out the irresponsible child in you? Now, write your insights in the north of the wheel.

EAST, or the right quadrant of your circle, is the place of the mind, reflecting ancient wisdom. The east is also the home of the *heyoka*, the sacred clown or court jester, always teasing and poking fun at established institutions and the status quo. The reflections presented by this direction can be incredibly profound, and it is important to always look at both sides of this "coin." Examine the "Power Statement" from the east. How do you think about power? Is power something that you understand? When you think of power, do you think of power over someone as a means of manipulation? Do you realize that your greatest power is in your own vulnerability? Now, write your insights in the east of the wheel.

Now look at your wheel in its wholeness. What is the teaching here? Is there a sense of balance? Do you need to focus more energy in one particular area of your life? Remember, you want to sit in the center of your own life-wheel to always be aware of where you are in relation to your physical world, your emotions, your spiritual life, and your mind. Living in the center of your own truth is living a life of balance and mastery.

In addition to drawing a circle on paper, you may want to build an actual wheel in which to do your work. By doing so, you can sit within or face the different directions as you journey around the circle. When building a sacred wheel, use a compass to determine true south, west, north, and east, placing a stone to represent each direction. As you place each stone, keep in mind the essence of that direction, calling forth the teachings that will present themselves to you there. This can be done in your home, in your yard, or out in the wilderness. What is important is that you find a place where you will be comfortable and will not be distracted while you work. Always approach this task with respect and honor, consecrating your sacred wheel with prayers of gratitude.

Horizontal and Vertical Movement

The wheel provides us with another important mirror. Enlightenment comes from the movement created by vertical consciousness, and the wheel can help us discover how we move or perhaps don't move around the wheel. Most of us spend a majority of our lives moving on a horizontal plane, a movement from west to east, or emotions to mind. In relationships, especially, we get stuck in the process of *"How I feel about what you think, and what you think about how I feel."* When we are judging ourselves, or anyone else for that matter, we are stuck in a horizontal movement.

Once in a while we move up to the north, the home of Spirit. We have moments where we connect with God through meditation, prayer, silence, nature, and acts of creation. These moments create vertical movement, and it is in this movement that we receive inspiration. When we bring the inspiration of the north into the south, we are manifesting it into physical form, breathing life into it. From this we may bring about an amazing scientific discovery, create a beautiful work of art, or realize a profound sense of peace and well-being that we are able to share with others. It is through this vertical consciousness that we find enlightenment and balance.

Point of View

Who you are in the world, your ability to love yourself and others, and how you accept your own greatness and power are all connected to your *point of view*. Your point of view is the composite picture created by all of the thoughts you have, the ideas you decide are true, your experiences, and how you interpret things in life. Your point of view creates your reality. Think of it as a filter, and everything you experience must move through this filter before you can relate to it. It is essential for you to really look at what thoughts, ideas, and truths make up the point of view that you filter your world through. Are these ideas still true for you? Some are, most likely, and may continue to be true for this lifetime and beyond. But I bet you will find ideas that no longer hold true. As you grow and evolve, you change. We all do. Be aware of perceiving life from a new point of view. As you become aware, focus this filter to open up to more spiritual abundance, love, and power in your life.

Affirmations

In the beginning was the word. Words are a sacred tool and an essential aspect to accessing love and power. In the process of the work you will be doing this coming year, you will discover truths that you may want to make your own. To make these truths a part of your point of view, create an *affirmation*, or a positive statement, about this truth. For example, to empower your relationship to Spirit and spiritual abundance, you might write something such as, *"I welcome the gifts of the Great Spirit and I am grateful."* When writing an affirmation, be sure you use present-tense verbs to bring this relationship into the current time. Avoid the use of negative words such as *no*, *not*, or *never*. Work with your statement until it is powerful, positive, and simple enough to remember.

Bodymind

I will ask you to work with your *bodymind* during the coming year. What I mean by this is to notice how your body is reacting or responding to an idea, situation, or person. Learning to read your physical response is part of returning to a life of harmony and balance. Try the example below.

Using whatever name you have for God or the Great Spirit or the Goddess, read the following statement and notice how your *bodymind* reacts or responds.

> *God is within me, and God is good.*
> *I am God, and God is me.*

Did you feel a connection to this statement in your physical body? Did you have a sensation such as warmth, coolness, or tingling? This is your *bodymind* responding to the statement.

Sacred Witness

Another term I will use is *sacred witness*. This is similar to sitting in the center of your own circle. In the place of the sacred witness, you can sit calmly, simply observing a storm as it swirls around you. It is from the place of the sacred witness that we listen and observe a person, experience, or situation without judgment. To know that you and God are one and that you are one with all of life is to be in the place of the sacred witness. Gaining awareness of your essential reality, you move into this place of sacred witness—creating a world of balance and harmony, a world of tenderness and understanding.

At some point during the course of your year-long journey, you will likely come face-to-face with something from your past that has prevented you from fully and completely expressing your love and living in your power. This could be an incident from your childhood or something that has happened more recently. This is the perfect time to move into your sacred witness, allowing these wounds to be healed. They are presenting themselves to you for a reason, and that reason is to be healed and woven into the wonderful and magical tapestry that is your life.

These are the tools I want you to learn to use. This workbook will provide a sacred record of your journey as you discover your own truths and record them here. Some ideas we will visit more than once. If you feel pulled to a particular thought, revisit it yourself. This workbook is about your journey to wholeness. I will give you guidance, mirror some ideas to you, and show you how to find the gateways within your own world. But your journey and the gifts you find along the way are your responsibility, and they belong to you. Own them proudly.

To engage yourself for a full year in personal exploration may appear to be a self-ish process. But it is necessary to be selfish to become self-aware, and ultimately it is a selfless act because we are, in fact, all one. I invite you to begin this process now, by reading and completing the following *Sacred Agreement*. I wish you success, power, and love on your journey.

Sacred Agreement

There is a magical wisdom inside you. When personal crossroads arrive in your life, how do you choose a direction? Where do you go inside yourself to find answers? As you begin this journey, know that in committing to this path, you will encounter both the gateways and the obstacles to enlightenment. The gateways are the gift of the Great Spirit. The real question is, who creates the obstacles in your life?

If you choose to accept my invitation to work with this book during the coming year, know that this is a journey of great joy and amazing challenges. I have carefully laid out this path for your journey. You will all walk the same path, but no two of you will have the same journey. That is the awesome power of the mystery. The mystery is beautiful, and the mystery is unknown. Along this path you will discover many splendid gifts that, like diamonds or precious gemstones, may require your care and attention. It is in the careful cutting and polishing of a stone that its beauty fully comes to light. There will be other gifts that may appear as obstacles. View each one carefully, for it is by knowing the obstacle and how it relates to you that you transform it into your ally. Until you truly see into the deepest shadows of your being, you will not be able to fully overcome your personal limitations.

You have found this book in your hands, and the mystery is now calling you forth. If you are willing to take your place within the circle of self-discovery and begin your journey toward spiritual mastery and balancing love and power, sign and date this page to acknowledge your commitment to the coming year of personal growth, enlightenment, and transformation.

I, _____ , agree to complete this process of self-discovery and healing. I also agree to let go of that which no longer serves me and to learn from the challenges before me. I will gently move whatever obstacles need to be moved, step into my power, and create my own reality, knowing that it is possible to move mountains when my intent declares it so.

Signature_____ Date_____

Week 1

Moving Around the Sacred Wheel

Reflection:

You manifest the jewel of your existence with every breath, with every day that you are alive.

Sacred Practice—Discovering Your Starting Point:

The wheel is not a tool for self-processing. It is, rather, a sacred tool for self-discovery. The wheel honors the process of living and the mystery of life. Begin this first week by working with the wheel to discover where you are in your life, to determine your point of view, and to learn which of the four directions is your home, or the direction that you feel closest to. Explore the following list of questions, and place your answers on the wheel to discover the starting point of your journey. Remember, life is fluid, everchanging, so just let the answers come. Do not try to think about what the answers should be or what you want them to be. Be honest with yourself. Listen to your own voice, and trust that where you are is truly perfect for you right now.

Look at the following questions and each time you answer yes to one of them, draw a symbol in the corresponding direction on the wheel. You may want to use a star or spiral, or even a simple dot.

SOUTH

1. Do you have a regular exercise routine?
2. Do you enjoy physical work and using your body?
3. Do you enjoy dancing?
4. Do you like to garden?
5. Do you like your body?

WEST

1. Are you an emotional person?
2. Are you comfortable expressing your emotions?
3. Do your emotions get you in trouble?
4. Do you remember your dreams?
5. Do you welcome change?

NORTH

1. Do you have a sense of oneness with all life?
2. Do you have a personal experience of your relationship to God or Spirit?
3. Are you aware of moments of inspiration?
4. Do you sense shifts in the energy around you?
5. Do you feel drawn to the mysteries of life?

EAST

1. Are you a logical person?
2. Are you mentally disciplined?
3. Do you question "why" before acting on someone else's decision?
4. Do you question authority?
5. Do you enjoy shaking up existing structures?

Look at the wheel in its entirety. Are the number of symbols balanced on the wheel? For example, do you find the same number of stars in each direction, or do you have 5 in the west (emotions), and only 2 or 3 in the other directions? Most of you will find at least one symbol in each direction, or you may not. Do not judge yourself on this. There is no right or wrong. This is about self-discovery.

One of the most profound aspects of the wheel is its ability to move us deeper and deeper into the mystery each time we explore the directions. This time, use your Personal Pages as we begin our journey around the sacred wheel again.

Starting in the SOUTH, the realm of the physical, the direction or place of manifestation, write about how you manifest yourself in the world physically.

Look at the WEST, the place of emotions, the direction of transformation, death, and rebirth. Write about your relationship with your emotions.

Look now to the NORTH, the direction of spirit, representing the strength and essence of your own spirit, and write about how you relate to God.

In the EAST, we find the mind, our connection to the old, wise one within. Write about your relationship with your own mind and the mental process.

Now that you have made your second journey around the wheel, consider this: People who relate most to the south love the physical realm and feel strongly connected to Mother Earth. They also may love having stones and crystals around them. Is this you?

Those drawn to the west, the emotions, are often dreamers both awake and asleep. West people are drawn to water and expansive open spaces with room to contemplate and dream. Dreamers can be incredibly productive when they understand how to manifest their dreams.

North people often have the ability to see energy in and around people or objects. They understand what it takes to be an adult in this world. They sense their own spiritual strength and connection.

In the east, we find the trickster and the wise one often in the same person. East people can be very mental and seem to be without emotion, trusting their mind and their ability to figure things out. They can also move quickly from one thought to the next and may be a challenge to keep up with. They can appear very serious, deep in thought, and in an instant, can turn around and poke fun at anything serious and seemingly important.

Now reread what you have written in your Personal Pages about your relationship to the directions. Notice how your *bodymind* reacts as you do this. What direction do you feel the strongest connection to? Ask yourself where you live on the sacred wheel. Place a symbol that represents *you* on this wheel. Remember, this work is about finding balance—balance between love and power, and balance between the four directions. Look at your wheel. What is it telling you? If you live in the south, look to the north, the natural point of balance for you. What is there? How do you relate to the direction that is directly across from you on the wheel? Continue writing in your Personal Pages about your discoveries.

Week 2

Sacred Practice—Creating a Place for Love and Power:

I have often said that for power to be present in your life, you must make a place inside you for power to live. The same holds true for love. To make a place within you for love and power to live, begin by looking at how you relate to both. As you answer the following questions, notice what is happening in your *bodymind*.

Take some time with this. Do not judge your responses; just let them flow. I know that it takes courage to really look at yourself. I also know that you have that courage. If you sense yourself beginning to edit your thoughts, stop writing, take a few slow, deep breaths, releasing any tension you feel in your body as you exhale. You may want to slowly stretch, tightening and relaxing your muscles, releasing any stress or energy knots you find. Then very gently move back to your journal work.

1. Using the wheel, I want you to look at, and write about, your relationship with power. Here are some questions to help you begin.

    — Where do you sense that power lives in your body?
    — How do you physically express power?
    — How do you physically experience power?
    — Are you comfortable with your physical power?
    — Do you express power through your emotions?
    — When you contemplate power, what emotions do you feel?
    — Are you afraid of power?
    — Are you afraid of what it means to be a person of power?
    — Do you fear the power of God?
    — Have you given away your power to God or to a spiritual teacher or guru?
    — Do you feel that power and spirit can coexist?
    — Do you trust the power of your mind?
    — What do you think about power?

2. Now continue using the wheel to explore and write about your relationship to love.

- Where do you sense love lives in your body?
- How do you physically express love?
- How do you physically experience love?
- Are you comfortable with your physical love?
- Do you express love through your emotions?
- When you contemplate love, what emotions do you feel?
- Are you afraid of love?
- Are you afraid of what it means to be a loving person?
- Do you experience the love of God?
- Do you hold back your love from God?
- What do you think about love?
- Does your mind sabotage your expression of love?

3. Where does power live in your body? When you have found the area in your body where power lives, take a moment and focus your intent there. Begin to sense or see a symbol that represents power within this area of your body. What color is this symbol? How large is it? Draw this symbol on your Personal Pages.

4. Where does love live in your body? When you have located the area in your body where love lives, take some time and focus your intent there. This time, begin to sense or see the symbol that represents love for you. What color is this symbol? How large is it? Again, draw this symbol on your Personal Pages.

5. What is the current relationship between love and power within your body? Is one larger or more defined than the other? Meditate on this and write in your Personal Pages about what you have just discovered.

Reflection:

Learning to love and accept yourself is the first step on the road to mastery.

Ideas to Contemplate:

1. We can all learn so much from each other. Take some time this week and find five people who you think have achieved a degree of mastery in some area. These are people who love themselves in a powerful way.

2. Ask at least two of them how they have achieved their level of mastery. Don't be shy. Anyone who loves and accepts themselves is not going to judge you. They will understand the importance of your journey. You may surprise yourself and begin a new, powerful, and nurturing relationship.

3. Pay attention to how they use their personal power in their own life, in their relationships, and in their work.

(We will be revisiting this teaching as we move through this year.)

Week 4

Reflection:

A person of power attains their goals and remains whole as a person. To truly have power, you must love yourself enough to live within the center of your own truth.

Ideas to Contemplate:

1. You are beginning to develop the strength and ability to see yourself through your own eyes. Now it is time to define what power means to you.

2. List five personal values or qualities that you consider important.

3. What five aspects or qualities about yourself are you proud of?

4. What are some accomplishments that you are proud of?

5. What does personal power mean to you?

Reflection:

Know that all of life is your mirror. Every situation contains a lesson for you, a challenge in some way, where your consciousness can become wrapped around that moment and a new vision can be brought to life. Once you live and understand this, you will begin to experience the fulfillment of mastery.

Ideas to Contemplate:

1. Pay attention this week and look for the mirrors in your life.

2. It is essential to look at every situation and every interaction with an open heart.

3. Be discerning, but without judgment.

4. Where were you open and discerning this week? What did you learn from the experience? How has this affected your point of view?

Week 6

Reflection:

To achieve balance and harmony in your life, you need an understanding of energy. What is energy? Energy is the whirling protons, electrons, and neutrons that produce friction and heat. The real questions is: "What creates the movement, the force, the life spirit?" God! Energy is life. Everything is made of energy, including you. Energy is power. If you don't truly understand that you are made of energy, that you are a moving life force that needs direction and intent, then you cannot express who you are in society in a meaningful way.

Ideas to Contemplate:

1. What is your definition of energy?

2. How do you find or receive direction in your life?

3. How do you gather your intent?

4. How do you express who you are in the world?

Week 7

Reflection:

To have a relationship with power, you have to sit with power. You have to give it your time. Power tests you always. It is a whole relationship with energy forces. Begin now to listen. Be aware of power sitting next to you waiting and wanting to be heard.

Ideas to Contemplate:

1. Pay attention. Power is always calling you, stalking you. I have heard so many amazing stories of how people started reading my work, wonderful tales of my books literally flying off the shelf and hitting someone on the head. They open the book and begin their journey.

2. Think back: How did you discover this journal or any of my other books that brought you to this path?

3. How has power been trying to get your attention?

4. Pay attention this week and be aware of when power is calling you.

Week 8

Reflection:

Home is the sacred garden of our own spirit—that place of serenity within each of us. You don't find paradise **out there.** *Paradise is a world where we live in the center of our own reality, knowing who we are. In this world of mastery, we are not afraid to take risks, to love one another, and to follow our dreams.*

Ideas to Contemplate:

1. Home is a reflection of how you honor yourself and how you love yourself. How does your home support you physically? Are you comfortable?

2. Do you feel good in your environment? Look around: Do you see beauty in your world?

3. Do you have a place in your home to meditate, to connect with God?

4. Can you focus and think clearly in your space? Clutter in a room can create clutter in your mind.

5. What changes are you willing to make in your home that will create a more loving and supportive environment? Begin them now.

Week 9

Reflection:

The circle provides an important focusing tool for understanding yourself. As you begin to understand yourself, you begin to heal yourself; and as you heal yourself, you can then take your power and heal the world around you. So we must heal our fear of taking our power. The well-being of our world depends on it.

Sacred Practice:

Using the Sacred Wheel, answer the following questions in each direction:

1. SOUTH—the place of the inner child: Is there any fear or anxiety from your childhood that is standing between you and your power today?

2. WEST—the place of the adolescent: Was it safe for you as a teenager to express your power? Does the "teenage rebel" within you still affect the way you use and express your power in the world?

3. NORTH—the place of the adult: How does the adult in you honestly feel about being powerful in the world?

4. EAST—the place of the old wise one: What are your fears or concerns about aging in a society where the elderly have their power dishonored?

(We will journey around this circle again next week,
looking at it from a place of love.)

Week 10

Reflection:

The circle provides an important focusing tool for understanding yourself. As you begin to understand yourself, you begin to heal yourself; and as you heal yourself, you can then take your love and heal the world around you. We must heal our fear of expressing and receiving love. The well-being of our world depends on it.

Sacred Practice:

Using the Sacred Wheel, answer the following questions in each direction:

1. SOUTH—the place of the inner-child: Is there any fear or anxiety from your childhood that is standing between you and fully experiencing love today?

2. WEST—the place of the adolescent: Was it safe for you as a teenager to express your love? Does the "awkward teenager" within you still affect the way you receive and express love in the world?

3. NORTH—the place of the adult: How does the adult in you honestly feel about being worthy of love?

4. EAST—the place of the old wise one: What are your fears or concerns about aging in a society where the elderly have their values and desires disregarded?

(Take a moment and review Weeks 9 and 10. Notice the similarities and the differences. Become aware of creating a place for love and power to live.)

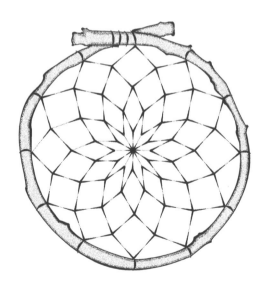

Week 11

Reflection:

*For you to be successful and powerful in your endeavors in **your** lifetime helps me to become successful and powerful in **my** lifetime. If we could learn the true anatomy of power, we could solve the environmental problems that are plaguing our planet. We could quell our riots. We could end our wars.*

Ideas to Contemplate:

1. Find someone whose success and power inspires you.

2. Let that person know what they have done for you.

3. Look at your successes and accomplishments. Have these acts inspired other people?

Sacred Practice—Power of Place:

Take a few moments to sit in quiet contemplation. Think of a place in nature in which you feel a special connection. Is it in the mountains, next to the ocean, by a river or a lake, in the desert, in a beautiful forest, or perhaps in an open meadow? If nothing comes to mind immediately, simply relax, take a nice deep breath, and just let your imagination guide you. This may be a place you discovered as a child or found in a photograph. You want this to be a place that has moved something within you.

Once you have this image, hold it in your mind's eye. Using your intention, focus on this image, as though you were stepping into a movie. Let your senses begin to experience this place of natural beauty and joy. What does it smell like? Are there flowers or the smell of dark, rich earth? Can you feel or sense the wind? What about the sun? Can you begin to sense its warmth, or is it, perhaps, evening? Is there a chill in the air that invigorates you? Can you see the moon reflecting off the water or through the trees? Explore your magic creation.

This place is a very special place for you. It is a place where you can store energy. It would be wonderful if you could actually visit this place at some time, but even if it is not a place you can physically go to, it is still a place where you have a special connection and you can use it to store energy and renew yourself anytime you need to.

Imagine moving a stream of light—a beautiful, pure, golden-white light—from your power center, near your solar plexus just below your navel, into this place in nature. Your energy can move into a mountain or a magnificent tree or a body of water, wherever it is you feel drawn. See this aspect of nature begin to radiate with your energy. Use your intent and focus while you continue this flow of energy. As you breathe in, know that you are bringing in energy. With each exhale, see this stream of energy flowing out from your power center and into this place in nature. With each breath you increase the flow of energy. Then, very gently, begin decreasing this energy flow, holding more of the light within you. Feel yourself being filled with this beautiful energy. Notice how you feel. This energy flow is unlimited, so you may feel even more energized, more focused than before you started. Sense with your *body-mind*. How is your body feeling?

Remember to return to this beautiful, nurturing place from time to time. If you are feeling tired or are having trouble focusing, take a moment and bring this place into your mind's eye. This time, however, see or sense the pure energy moving from the mountain or the water back into your power center, your solar plexus. Breathe in deeply and experience yourself being renewed and revitalized.

Continue from time to time to store your energy in this magical place. Your ability to succeed at this depends on your will and focus. Use your will to bring forth the picture of what you want in your life. It is your intent that empowers your will and brings these pictures, your vision, into manifestation. This requires practice and learning to trust yourself.

Ideas to Contemplate:

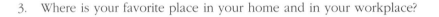

1. Where do you feel your most powerful?

2. Where do you feel your most peaceful?

3. Where is your favorite place in your home and in your workplace?

4. Where is your favorite place in nature?

5. Is there a piece of music or a work of art that reminds you of the place of power you have just discovered?

6. Do you have an aspect of nature within your home and workplace? Plants, pets, crystals or rocks, even a photograph of nature, will remind you of your oneness, your connectedness, to all of life.

Week 13

Reflection:

Love is the energy that brings our existence to life. It animates everything that we are, everything that we do, and all that we create. Nature reflects the perfect balance of love and power, and reminds us of our intimate connection to all of life. While we may think we can control or direct nature, in the end, it is nature that redefines us.

Ideas to Contemplate:

1. Look around your personal environment. How do you have nature represented in your home? In your workplace?

2. It is important to find your place of renewal. Where in your environment do you feel your energy or spirit renewed?

Week 14

Sacred Practice—Mirror Exercise:

What is keeping you from fully expressing your love?

Look deeply at this question and your answers to it. Create your own affirmation to transform your ability to fully express love. For instance, if you discover that your do not express love because you get embarrassed, you would write something like: *I freely express love*, or *I am comfortable expressing love*. Say your affirmation out loud to yourself in the mirror. Look deeply into your own eyes, deeply into the eyes of that loving person looking back at you. And say your affirmation for love. Close your eyes for a moment and visualize yourself as fully self-expressed, the embodiment of love. Open your eyes again and look at the loving person looking back at you. Say your affirmation again. Keep this affirmation with you all week. Post it next to the bathroom mirror, inside a desk drawer, inside your car, on the refrigerator. Keep it alive by surrounding yourself with it. Write about this experience in your Personal Pages. From this point of view, how has your expression of love shifted?

Week 15

Reflection:

A person of power attains their goals and remains whole as a person. To truly have power, you must first love yourself enough to stay in your own center of truth.

Ideas to Contemplate:

1. Trading away aspects of yourself that you know to be true, in order to please another, will drain your personal power and your happiness. Are you living true to yourself and honoring who you know yourself to be?

2. Where in your life do you feel your energy being drained?

3. When you feel off balance or drained of energy, you may have attained an immediate goal or some experience of instant gratification, but you have traded away an aspect of your soul.

Week 10

Reflection:

Every relationship in your life provides an opportunity for spiritual growth,
a possibility to experience more love in your life.

Ideas to Contemplate:

1. This week, be aware of the casual relationships that you encounter and look for the spiritual gifts and teachings each one offers.

2. In your neighborhood, do you have a sense of community where you live?

3. In your work environment, everything you do is the expression of spirit. How do your relationships at work serve your spiritual growth?

4. What are the spiritual gifts from your family and friends?

Week 17

Reflection:

Always remember that the situation or person with the ability to upset you the most, to pull you off center, is your greatest teacher.

Ideas to Contemplate:

1. Use the paradigm created by the Sacred Wheel to move into the mystery of this teaching for the next four weeks. Examine the many aspects of the south this week.

2. Look at your physical life, your environment, your health, your body and what you do in the world. What situation or person has the ability to upset you the most?

3. Who or what throws you off center and out of balance?

4. Sit in the center of this wheel and look to the south. Ask your *bodymind* and your inner wisdom what teaching this is bringing you.

5. If you sense a weakness in yourself, move into it and learn where your strength is.

6. How can you stay centered in the presence of this person or situation?

7. How do you need to shift your point of view to accomplish this?

8. Center yourself in your power. Now release your need to be distracted from your greatness.

9. How can you express yourself in a more powerful way in the physical world?

Week 18

Reflection:

Always remember that the situation or person with the ability to upset you the most, to pull you off center, is your greatest teacher.

Ideas to Contemplate:

1. Continue using the paradigm created by the Sacred Wheel to move into the mystery of this teaching for the next three weeks. Examine the many aspects of the west this week.

2. Look at your emotions, how you emotionally relate to the world around you. Who or what can throw you off center? When you criticize yourself, whose voice is it that you hear? Remember the last time you felt you were living in emotional chaos. Who or what created the chaos?

3. Sit in the center of this wheel and look to the west. Ask your *bodymind* and your inner wisdom what teaching this is bringing you.

4. How can you stay centered and emotionally focused in the presence of this person or situation?

5. How can you release your desire to be seduced away from your own personal power?

6. How do you need to shift your point of view to accomplish this?

7. How can you live powerfully in your emotions and stay focused and centered at the same time?

Week 19

Reflection:

Always remember that the situation or person with the ability to upset you the most, to pull you off center, is your greatest teacher.

Ideas to Contemplate:

1. Continue using the paradigm created by the Sacred Wheel to move into the mystery of this teaching for the next two weeks. Examine the many aspects of the north this week.

2. Look at your spiritual life and your relationship to God or the Great Spirit. Who or what can shake your faith? What situation or person has the ability to make you feel disconnected from life? To feel abandoned by God?

3. Sit in the center of this wheel and look to the north. Ask your *bodymind* and your inner wisdom what teaching this is bringing you.

4. How can you stay centered in the presence of this person or situation?

5. How do you need to shift your point of view to accomplish this?

6. How can you express your spiritual self in a healing, powerful, and creative way?

Week 20

Reflection:

Always remember that the situation or person with the ability to upset you the most, to pull you off center, is your greatest teacher.

Ideas to Contemplate:

1. Continue using the paradigm created by the Sacred Wheel to move into the mystery of this teaching for the next week. Examine the many aspects of the east this week.

2. Look at your mental life, the incredibly powerful world of the mind. Where do you find yourself doubting your own ability to discern? Who or what creates doubt in your mind? In what circumstances do you find yourself spiraling downward into a mental abyss of your own creation?

3. Sit in the center of this wheel and look to the east. Ask your *bodymind* and your inner wisdom what teaching this is bringing you.

4. How can you stay centered in the presence of this person or situation?

5. How do you need to shift your point of view to accomplish this?

6. How can you express your thoughts and your mental acumen in a more powerful way in the world?

Week 21

Sacred Practice—Mirror Exercise:

What is keeping you from fully expressing your power?

Look deeply at this questions and your answer to it. Create your own affirmation to transform your ability to fully express power. For instance, if you discover that you do not express power because you are afraid people will not like you, you would write something like: *It is safe for me to express my power,* or *The way I express my power attracts people to me*. Say your affirmation out loud to yourself in the mirror. Look deeply into your own eyes, deeply into the eyes of that powerful person looking back at you. And say your affirmation for power. Close your eyes for a moment and visualize yourself as fully self-expressed, the embodiment of power. Open your eyes again and look at the powerful person looking back at you. Say your affirmation again. Keep this affirmation with you all week. Post it next to the bathroom mirror, inside a desk drawer, inside your car, on the refrigerator. Keep it alive by surrounding yourself with it. Write about this experience in your Personal Pages. From this point of view, how has your expression of power shifted?

Reflection:

Defining your self-worth and your intent develops your point of view. Power comes from a sense of focus, well-being, and health—all of which emanate from maintaining a balanced point of view in the world.

Ideas to Contemplate:

1. I speak often of the importance of developing a point of view in your life, taking the time to consciously understand the perspective by which you view life.

2. How did your childhood and early life influence your point of view?

3. How do your relationships affect this perspective?

4. Has your point of view shifted since you began this journal?

5. Describe these changes and how it is reflected in your life.

6. How do you view POWER from this new perspective?

7. How do you view LOVE from this new perspective?

Week 23

Reflection:

Just before the moment when the flow begins in the opposite direction, the flow of letting go and release, there comes a superior moment in your life. A moment is visited upon you like no other. It is a moment of stillness, when you wait, and you listen, and you feel the essence of your creation, the essence of your God.

Ideas to Contemplate:

1. The experience of oneness and of separation are both teachings that bring you to mastery.

2. Describe an experience of oneness that brought you to a moment of stillness.

3. Describe an experience of separation that brought you to a moment of stillness.

4. What do these two experiences have in common?

5. Look for moments like these this week, and write about them in your Personal Pages.

Reflection:

For there to be beauty in your life, you must first make a place for beauty to live.

Ideas to Contemplate:

1. Making a place within your life for beauty and joy to live is essential to your soul and will illumine your existence. Take a moment each day to find the beauty and joy in your life. Write about these moments in your Personal Pages.

2. Bring flowers, or even just one flower, into your home or work place. How does this make you feel?

3. Where do you find beauty in life?

Reflection:

When you really love yourself, you naturally express who you are in the world.
You do not hide your light under a bushel.

Ideas to Contemplate:

1. Name five people who naturally express their essence in the world.
   - What is it that you admire most about them?
   - Why are people attracted to them?
   - What do these people have in common with each other?
   - What do you have in common with them?

2. Write about a time in your life when you truly loved yourself and allowed the world to see your natural magnificence and beauty.

3. What are five things you are willing to do to express the truth of who you are in the world? Begin this week to do at least one of them.

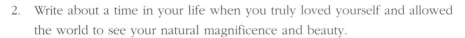

Reflection:

Love and power must go hand in hand. They are inexorably linked. One without the other is like a right side without the left. When love is felt inwardly but there is an absence of power, the love remains dormant, unable to reach out and affect the world at large.

Sacred Practice:

I want you to look again at where love and power live within you. Focus on seeing or sensing the symbol that represents each of these energies for you.

Take a moment and close your eyes. Let your breath become soft and deep. Allow your intention to move throughout your body and find where love lives within you. It may be in the same place that you found it last time, or it may have moved. Has it changed color? What does it feel like now? Is it larger than it was? What is the symbol you see or sense here? Use your Personal Pages to describe what you have found.

Now, close your eyes once again and let your breath become soft and deep. Allow your intention to move throughout your body and find where power lives within you. It may be in the same place that you found it last time or it may have moved. Has it changed color? What does it feel like now? Is it larger than it was? What is the symbol you see or sense there? Use your Personal Pages to describe what you have found.

Notice how these two energies balance each other. Do you need to bring in more power to balance the love or the other way around? Love without power will be ineffective, and power without love can be harsh.

Where are you in your journey to balance love and power? Write about this in your Personal Pages.

Reflection:

The alpha wolf does not usually have to prove her position, except by her presence. Occasionally she may be challenged, and then she has to fight. But an alpha wolf is prepared to fight, and because of being prepared to fight, she usually does not have to. This quality has to do with her mettle, the steel that is inside her, holding her up, making her strong—and others sense and respect it.

Ideas to Contemplate:

1. Do you sense or feel a knot in your stomach when you think about building your power?

2. In your family of origin, who was the alpha wolf? Has that relationship changed?

3. Who in your life today is the alpha wolf? Is it you?

4. What are the traits or qualities of this person that you admire most?

5. Are you uncomfortable or nervous around this person? Why?

6. There is an important lesson about power for you in this relationship. Move into your *bodymind* and discover what this teaching is.

Week 28

Reflection:

It is time to redefine power, to expand our concept of what being powerful really means. True power is love. It is not power over someone. It is everyone, all of us, standing together in a circle, building power side-by-side. As I build my power, I create a mirror, a reflection of power that you can use to build your power. It is not rivalry, but rather healthy competition—a world where I inspire you and you inspire me; and together we create a world of healthy, interdependent, creative people.

Ideas to Contemplate:

1. Take some time and really think about how you now define power.

2. What is the difference between rivalry and healthy competition?

3. How has your point of view shifted? Write about this in your Personal Pages.

Reflection:

Be a star in your own world. Find the intent, find the courage, find whatever it takes, but make the effort and become a shining star.

Ideas to Contemplate:

1. List five things you do that give you joy simply in the act of doing them. This could be anything from washing the windows of your home, to running a local marathon, to volunteering in your community, or being successful at your job. What matters, most is that you give this activity the best of yourself and, in return, you realize your own gifts.

2. What did you want to be when you were five years old? Remember back to that time in your life. Why did you want to become this type of person?

3. What did you want to be when you were ten years old? Remember back to that time in your life. Why did you want to become this type of person?

4. Are you doing any of these things now? If not, why did your dreams change?

5. Are you living your dream today, or someone else's?

Week 30

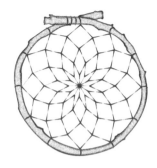

Reflection:

Spiritual masters know when to hold their energy and when to release energy. This innate sense of timing is essential to living a life of balance. If you can sense when to let go of situations that drain you and no longer serve anyone, you hold the key that unlocks the door to true skill and mastery.

Ideas to Contemplate:

1. When you hold on, or stay in a relationship that is draining your energy, you are actually keeping the wound of this relationship alive and growing. Look back at relationships in your life and see if you can find a pattern. Do you leave early, before the relationship becomes real, or do you hang on even though you know the relationship no longer serves you? Do you do both?

2. Are you in a relationship now that you are hanging on to?

3. We also hold on to our point of view in life, our need to be right. When have you held on to a particular perspective or view about something even though it no longer served you or you knew it was no longer true for you?

4. Look at your point of view right now—what you think about yourself, others, your work, your spiritual practices, your sense of oneness in the world. Are you holding on to a particular idea or attitude that really does not serve you? Did you let go of someone or something that you now realize was truly important to you?

Week 31

Welcoming Abundance—Part I

Reflection:

If you have chosen to live from a position of true personal power, you will naturally accept abundance into your life to nourish your love-power connection.

Ideas to Contemplate:

1. Take some time and consider your relationship to abundance.

2. Do you welcome the flow of money in your life?

3. Do you feel your body constrict or tighten when you have to think about or deal with money—for example, paying bills or collecting money that is owed to you?

4. Are you afraid of having money, or do you trust yourself with money?

5. In the space below, write out five statements about your relationship to abundance and money.

Now reread the five statements you just wrote about your relationship to abundance, but this time read them as statements about your relationship to God, to Spirit.

Your relationship with abundance and money is a spiritual teaching, not a material one. It is not about money. It is, in truth, about your tendency to stop the flow of energy through your body and your life. Everything we experience in this life is a spiritual teaching. What matters is paying attention so that we don't miss the lesson. Paying attention is staying present in the moment. The gifts of Spirit exist only in the present moment.

Now write an affirmation or positive statement about how you want your relationship with Spirit and abundance to be. Check to be sure you use present-tense verbs to bring this relationship into the present time. Avoid the use of negative words such as *no*, *not*, or *never*. Work with your statement until it is powerful, positive, and simple enough to remember. This is your affirmation for abundance of spirit as well as money.

Week 32
Welcoming Abundance—Part II

Reflection:

Enlightenment is found in the movement between inspiration and the manifestation of that inspiration.

Sacred Practice—The Abundance-of-Spirit Wheel:

Your creativity, your money, your evolvement, and your relationships are all a direct reflection of your willingness, openness, and ability to bring your intuitions from spirit into manifestation. This week, you will be working with the Abundance-of-Spirit Wheel.

Begin in the south, the place of the physical world and the child. For most of us, there were one or two key moments or events in our childhood that have become the foundation for how we experience abundance, money, and our self-worth. Take some time, relax, and breathe deeply. Now allow these moments to come forward in your memory. Write about these childhood experiences in your Personal Pages. Has this experience set up a pattern in your adult relationship to money and abundance?

The Abundance-of-Spirit Wheel

NORTH

Why do you shun
the gifts of Spirit?

EAST

Do you, with
mentation,
accumulate
wealth rather
than from the
heart create a
flow in the
Sacred
Giveaway?

WEST

Are you
emotionally
prepared to
accept money?

SOUTH

What event in your childhood
has created how you
relate to money?

For example, the experience may have left you with a sense of not being worthy of having money. Or you may have thought that if you got what you wanted, someone else would have to go without. Remember, this was experienced from the perspective of a young child. Look at how this has had an effect on the way you experience money and abundance. Is this a point of view that you are now choosing to shift to a new perspective or point of view?

Focus on the original experience from your childhood. Notice where you feel it in your body. There may be a place within your body where you will feel or sense a tightening or a denseness. With your intent, sense, see, or imagine a beam of pure golden-white light flowing into that area. Notice any thoughts or feelings that come as you release this blocked energy, and note them in your Personal Pages.

In the west, look at your emotional response to the subject of abundance and money. Do you feel emotionally prepared to have money? Do you trust yourself to have money and still be true to your values and friends? Are you afraid to trust Spirit to provide you with what you need and more? How do you feel about people who have enormous amounts of money? How do you feel about people who have less money than you? Look at how this has had an effect on the way you experience money and abundance. Don't edit yourself. Let your emotions flow into your Personal Pages.

Now, focus on where these emotions live in your body. Again, you will sense or experience an area where your body feels tight or stressed. With your intent, sense,

see, or imagine a beam of pure golden-white light flowing into that area. Notice any thoughts or feelings that come as you release this blocked energy. Continue your journal work.

In the north, it is important to be consciously open to the inspiration and gifts of Spirit. Do you have an intimate relationship with God? Do you spend time opening yourself to the inspiration of Spirit? If not, why? Are you willing to trust Spirit? Do you think that you can't be spiritual and have money? Are you concerned that money will become your God? Are you willing to trust the inspirations from Spirit? Look at how this has had an effect on the way you experience money and abundance, and write about this relationship.

Move into your body and focus on your sense of spiritual abundance in your life. Notice where you feel it in your body. There may be a place within your body where you will feel or sense a tightening or a denseness. You may see symbols or colors, so make note of anything that comes into your mind's eye. With your intent, sense, see, or imagine a beam of pure golden-white light flowing into that area. Notice any thoughts or feelings that come as you release this blocked energy, and record them in your Personal Pages.

In the east, look at whether you try to accumulate wealth with mental activity, allowing your mind to take control. What are the thoughts or fears that you have about poverty? Again, look at your willingness to trust Spirit. If you are hearing negative messages, where did you first hear them? Whose voice was it? And is the message really true for you today? Look at how this has had an effect on the way you experience money and abundance, and write about this in your Personal Pages.

Focus on any thoughts of poverty or lack that come up in your mind, and notice where you feel it in your body. There may be a place within your body where you will feel or sense a tightening or a denseness. With your intent, sense, see, or imagine a beam of pure golden-white light flowing into that area. Notice any thoughts or feelings that come as you release this blocked energy, and note them in your Personal Pages.

It is through your personal discoveries in moving around the wheel and looking at each direction that you begin to create a place within you for abundance to live.

Welcoming Abundance—Part III

Reflection:

Each experience in your life is a teacher, holding a mirror up to you so you can learn.

Ideas to Contemplate:

I have often said that my teachers refer to this great Mother Earth as a schoolhouse, and that we have all come here to learn. If you refuse to look into the mirrors that life presents to you, then you may very well miss your lessons. Every aspect of your life, from the family you were born and raised in, to the family and friends you create as an adult, provide mirrors for you. Your work can provide you with an extraordinary amount of information about who you are in this life. Likewise, the way you play and relax can contribute to your growth and evolvement. But you have to pay attention. The Universe will always provide you with what you need, whether that is an opportunity to bring money into your life right when you need it, or a seemingly difficult relationship that supports you in smoothing out some of your own rough spots and edges.

The Universe, Spirit, God will always provide both the obstacles and the gateways that are necessary on your path of heart toward self-realization and mastery.

There are four truths about the energy of abundance that I want you to contemplate. Write about these truths in your Personal Pages to discover how these ideas or concepts live within your being.

1. The first truth is that the universe really does provide us with exactly what we need to move forward on our path toward enlightenment. Are you willing to live in a place of trust, knowing and accepting that all of your physical, emotional, and spiritual needs will be met?

2. The second truth expands from the first. There are unlimited opportunities from which to learn in this life. Are you willing to be open to receiving the infinite abundance of Spirit through the gifts of money, health, and joyous relationships?

3. The third truth is simple. Abundance lives in a grateful heart. Do you live life with an attitude of gratitude?

4. The fourth truth: In this universe there is an unlimited abundance of love. If you develop an ability to love the process of life, to love the mystery, then abundance will flow freely in your life. Are you willing to love all of life?

The Sacred Giveaway Wheel

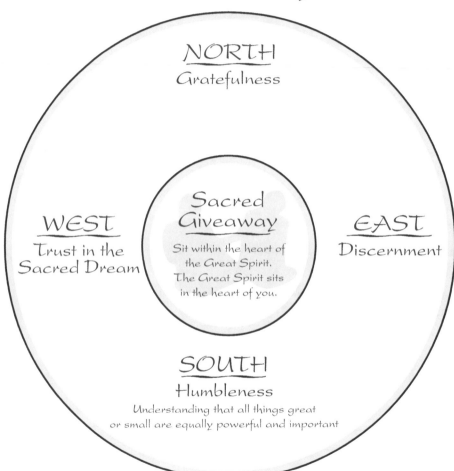

NORTH

Gratefulness

WEST

Trust in the
Sacred Dream

Sacred
Giveaway

Sit within the heart of
the Great Spirit.
The Great Spirit sits
in the heart of you.

EAST

Discernment

SOUTH

Humbleness

Understanding that all things great
or small are equally powerful and important

Week 34

Welcoming Abundance—Part IV

Reflection:

Life is a process of expansion within your mind and within your heart. Learn to live within this process, and abundance will be yours.

Sacred Practice: The Sacred Giveaway Wheel

Before we go on, I want to address the use of language. I am using the word *process,* and I write about "living within the process." When I speak about living within the process, I am referring to the ability of living within the mystery as it unfolds, living with the continual acceptance and increasing awe for the beauty and wonder that is life. I am not speaking about the therapeutic act of "processing," or said another way, moving inch by inch through the thoughts, feelings, and emotions associated with an issue. I know that as a therapeutic tool it can be valuable, but I also see people becoming addicted to the constant need to divert themselves by picking apart the beauty and the mystery of life, questioning every nuance, every thought and action to find the core problem or wound.

It is important to face your wounds and to embrace the shadow, but it is even more essential to work with them and then move through the wound or shadow to the other side and back into life and the light. It is the movement from the pain or shadow and back into the light that brings you to splendid moments of illumination. In my school of sacred arts, we refer to this as a "conscious act of course correction."

Most of us will set a goal and start off on our journey. As we go, we may get sidetracked by doubt or fear or some other form of self-sabotage. This often occurs when we come face-to-face with a personal wound or our shadow side. A conscious act of course correction involves the realization that we are off course, and the willingness to look directly at the wound or the shadow that has pulled us away from our target. We face this wound directly, we heal it, and we then make a conscious act to step back onto our path. It is with this movement that we experience enlightenment and illumination. At times, this movement can be as simple as letting go of the need to make something happen, and returning yourself to the stillness at your own center of truth and beauty.

One of the best ways to bring yourself back to center, back on course, is to work with the Sacred Giveaway Wheel and to live with a grateful heart. I want you to begin this week's work by sitting in the center of this wheel, contemplating what it means to sit within the heart of God and what it means to you that God sits within your heart.

Close your eyes and take several deep, even breaths. Sense, feel, or imagine what it is like to know with every cell and fiber of your being that you are sitting within the heart of God, that you are in the center of all that is. Stay within this experience and focus on the presence of God within your heart. Feel the awesome connection of this presence within you. With each breath, expand your sense of this experience. You are sitting within the center of your power, and you are sitting within the center of the love and power of all life.

Then look at one of the teachings from the south, humbleness. Write about an understanding that all things great or small are equally powerful and important. Do you ever judge yourself as being less important than someone or something else? Do you think that you are more important than someone or something else? How do you experience humbleness in your life?

Notice how your *bodymind* responds to this teaching. If there is an area of your body that is tense or tight, focus your intent in that area and ask your body why it is stressed by the idea of being humble. We all need or want to feel special in some way in our life. Does your need to be special interfere with your own path of enlightenment? Does it come from a place of pain and self-sabotage? Look at how this has had an effect on the way you experience life and spiritual abundance. Write about your discoveries.

There may be a place within your body where you will feel or sense a tightening or a denseness. With your intent, sense, see, or imagine a beam of pure golden-white light flowing into that area. Notice any thoughts or feelings that come as you release this blocked energy, and write about them in your Personal Pages.

Moving to the west, look at what you experience emotionally when you consider trusting the mystery, the Sacred Dream. If you have doubt or fear, where does it come from? What was the experience that placed that doubt in your mind? Is the doubt or fear real, or was it created within your imagination? Remember, the imagination is incredibly powerful. What you imagine can be as real for you as any physical experience. You can use this tool, your imagination, to open yourself up or to close yourself down. It is your choice. Look at how this has had an effect on the way you experience life and spiritual abundance. Write in your Personal Pages about this relationship.

Focus on your emotional energy. There may be a place within your body where you will feel or sense a tightening or a denseness. With your intent, sense, see, or imagine a beam of pure golden-white light flowing into that area. Notice any thoughts or feelings that come as you release this blocked energy, and note them in your Personal Pages.

North, as you know, is the place of Spirit. Do you live with a sense of gratitude? Spend some time this week cultivating your appreciation for the amazing experience called life. Use the following exercise to expand your perception of oneness and increase your gratitude. Look around, and for whatever you notice—the sky, a tree, the sidewalk or a car—repeat the following, using your own word for God, the Great Spirit, or the Goddess.

God is in the sky, and I am one with the sky and I am grateful.
God is in this tree, and I am one with this tree and I am grateful.
God is in the car, and I am one with the car and I am grateful.

Notice how your energy builds as you continue doing this exercise. Repeat this work each day to build your sense of oneness and gratitude to Spirit. Write in your Personal Pages about your relationship with Spirit. There may be a place within your body where you will feel or sense a tightening or a denseness. With your intent, sense, see, or imagine a beam of pure golden-white light flowing into that area. Notice any thoughts or feelings that come as you release this blocked energy, and record them in your Personal Pages.

In the east, I want you to look at discernment and the choices you make to hold yourself back. What are you clinging to and afraid to let go of, even though you know in your heart and in your mind that it no longer serves you? Discernment, not judgment, is the result of loving yourself and trusting your own power. But remember, discernment is not about throwing your hands in the air and charging ahead without a plan. Discernment is looking at what you truly want in life, what your passion is, doing an act of power, and preparing yourself to accomplish this. Find your target, carefully take aim, and then, when you know the time is right, let your arrows fly. Use this year and the work within this journal to build your intent, readying yourself with both love and power to hit the target.

Focus on discernment. How have you been holding yourself back? There may be a place within your body where you will feel or sense a tightening or a denseness. Now, look at what you are ready to let go of. With your intent, sense, see, or imagine a beam of pure golden-white light flowing into that area. Notice any thoughts or feelings that come as you release this blocked energy, and note them in your Personal Pages.

Remember, anytime you feel alone, sit in the center of this wheel and meditate on the truth that you are sitting within the heart of the Great Spirit and that the Great Spirit sits within your heart. Connect with the sense of love that is within your heart, allowing it to expand with each breath.

Week 35

Reflection:

How you express your power helps define your reality.

Ideas to Contemplate:

1. Does your concern for how you look overshadow who you are?

2. How can anger be creative? How does anger or jealousy affect your power?

3. If your life is an act of beauty, then what is there to be jealous of?

4. Who creates the obstacles to personal power in your life?

Reflection:

*The first lesson of power, and also of love, is that we are all alone. We view the world as **"me"** and **"them."** We have all experienced feeling left out or being different from the others around us. It is now time to appreciate the differences and to love the part that is uniquely you.*

Sacred Practice:

This week I want you to look at what makes you feel different and alone. I want you to celebrate this uniqueness and love that which is special about yourself.

1. Begin in the south and look at your physical existence, your body, your home, and your environment. What is different and unique? What has created your sense of separation? How can you heal this? From this new point of view, are you able to celebrate your uniqueness and to love that which is special about yourself?

2. Then in the west, look at your emotions, your sense of well-being. How do you feel about your life? What is different and unique? What feeling or emotion creates your sense of separation? How can you heal this? From this new point of view, are you able to celebrate your uniqueness and to love that which is special about yourself?

3. In the north, look at your relationship to God and your spiritual life. What is different and unique? What has created your sense of separation from God? Do you feel separate from others spiritually? How can you heal this? From this new point of view, are you able to celebrate your uniqueness and to love that which is special about yourself?

4. Finally, in the east, look at your thoughts and how you think about yourself. What is different and unique about how you think? What has created your thoughts of separation? How can you heal them? From this new point of view, are you able to celebrate your uniqueness and to love that which is special about yourself?

5. Create a party for yourself and your friends. Celebrate each unique being at the party!

Reflection:

Enlightened beings such as Jesus or Buddha are masters of love and power. They are masters of energy, and they understand that the source of all energy is ever-present and constant. This same source of energy is ever-present and constant within you. Become like a piece of hollow bamboo with the wind blowing through it. Energy flows just as the wind flows.

Ideas to Contemplate:

1. In what area of your life do you become like hollow bamboo and allow energy to flow?

2. Take some time to consider each of the following relationships that apply to you. Notice how your *bodymind* responds to the different elements. Where does your body tense up? Is it when you think about a friend whom you haven't seen recently because you passed on some gossip about him or her to

another friend? Use your Personal Pages to write about how you sense the flow of energy within you as you focus on these different people and experiences.

— Partner/Spouse, boyfriend/girlfriend, children, parents, siblings, grandparents, and other relatives. Don't forget blended families with stepparents, siblings, and children. And the exes—husbands, wives, and in-laws. Also, friends, co-workers, your boss—and don't forget any exes here that you still have some upset or judgments about.

3. Now look at other areas of your life. Again, notice how you respond, and explore these feelings in your Personal Pages.

— Work/career, creativity, money, physical health, having fun.

Week 38

Reflection:

Once we can see love as a fluid state of receptivity within our own hearts, then we can send it outward so that it touches all of those around us.

Ideas to Contemplate:

1. Describe at least one event in your life that has filled you with love—for example, taking the time to enjoy a sunset, looking at a work of art, being with someone you love, and so on.

2. Describe an occurrence when you sensed or felt love moving from you into the world in a conscious and healing way—for example, playing with a child, volunteering to help in your community, picking up litter, and so on.

3. How does being fluid affect your point of view in life? Write about how it feels to experience the flow of love.

Reflection:

Given the extraordinary stress of 20th-century life, love and power often seem to be opposing concepts. In truth, they are not. One is the reflection or shadow of the other, and each without the other is incomplete. Once we are able to recognize our personal power and imbue it with love, the glow emanating from our sense of well-being will automatically illuminate the environment around us.

Ideas to Contemplate:

1. How does love reflect power in your life?

2. How does power reflect love in your life?

3. Does love live within the shadow of power in your life?

4. Does power live under the shadow of love in your life?

Reflection:

When you heal the dis-ease in your spirit, you will discover that you have renewed your physical health as well. From this new point of view, you will innately under-stand the balance of love and power and the flow of energy. The contentment of the soul becomes reflected in our bodies as a glowing state of health and an absence of illness.

Ideas to Contemplate:

1. How do you comfort your soul?

2. What is your point of view regarding your own physical well-being and comfort?

3. What is your point of view regarding your own spiritual well-being?

Week 41

Reflection:

True power is love. An essential aspect of power is, in part, the true understanding of the spiritual energy that flows through all beings.

Ideas to Contemplate:

1. How do you bring inspiration and guidance into your life?

2. Describe how you create an act of vertical consciousness.

3. Are you manifesting this inspiration in your life?

4. Do you allow the energy of spirit to flow through you? It is this movement that opens you to healing and transformation.

Reflection:

To have personal power, it is essential to understand the power of failure. Failure brings a very powerful teaching with it—that is, if you are willing to look into the mirror your failures will provide you. If you stand as a victim and look into this mirror, the reflection will seduce you into another failure, as there is a great pull to slide backwards and regress to the status quo. But if you stand in the center of your own circle, your own power, and look into the reflection presented by the failure, you can learn a most powerful lesson. You can learn to succeed and move forward.

Ideas to Contemplate:

1. At what endeavors do you want to be successful?

2. Why do you want to succeed with these particular aspects?

3. Describe what your success would look like. What would be the results of your success?

4. How would this success change your life?

Reflection:

If you want power, you have to make a place inside you for power to live.

Sacred Practice:

In a journey toward love and power, it is essential to acknowledge your accomplishments along the way. Use the sacred wheel to discover where you are creating a place inside you for power to live. In each direction, begin with acknowledging what gifts you are discovering. Then, look to see what other wounds you may want to heal now.

Look back over your journey thus far. Beginning in the south, examine how you are shifting or healing your physical world and, in so doing, creating a place for power to live. Is there something else to heal in the south?

Now move to the west, where your emotions live. What is changing and what has healed? Are you able to use the energy of your emotions without being controlled by them? Is there something else to heal in the west?

Turn to the north. How is your relationship to spirituality and power shifting? How much spiritual power are you willing to receive? Is there something else to heal in the north?

Finally, in the east, ask yourself what is shifting and changing. What is your relationship to your mind? Who is in charge of your thoughts? Is there something else to heal in the east?

Review the wheel in its entirety. Is there a sense of balance? Have you done more work in one particular direction? Do you need to do a little more work in another? Use this valuable tool to move yourself into the place of the sacred witness, where you can clearly see yourself without judgment. This exercise can be one of profound self-discovery and healing. Acknowledge yourself for the movement you are creating in your life, and embrace the opportunity of continuing the healing process you have begun.

(We will journey around this circle again next week,
looking at it from a place of love.)

Reflection:

If you want love, you have to make a place inside you for love to live.

Sacred Practice:

In a journey toward love and power, it is essential to acknowledge your accomplishments along the way. Use the sacred wheel to discover where you are creating a place inside you for love to live. In each direction, begin with acknowledging what gifts you are discovering. Then look to see what other wounds you may want to heal now. This journey is about peeling back the layers of our misconception and unveiling our own truth and beauty.

Look back over your journey thus far. Beginning in the south, examine how you are shifting or healing your physical world, and in so doing, creating a place for love to live. Is there something else to heal in the south?

Move to the west, where your emotions live. What is changing and what has healed? Are you able to use the energy of your emotions to express love? Is there something else to heal in the west?

Turn to the north. How is your relationship to spirituality and self-love shifting? How much spiritual love are you willing to receive? Is there something else to heal in the north?

Finally, in the east, ask yourself what is shifting and changing. What is your relationship to your mind? Who is in charge of your thoughts? Are you beginning to love your mind? Is there something else to heal in the east?

Review the wheel in its entirety. Is there a sense of balance? Have you done more work in one particular direction? Do you need to do a little more work in another? Use this valuable tool to move yourself into the place of the sacred witness, where you can clearly see yourself without judgment. This exercise can be one of profound self-discovery and healing. Acknowledge yourself for the movement you are creating in your life, and embrace the opportunity of continuing the healing process you have begun.

Reflection:

Goodness, integrity, and wisdom already exist within your spirit, but you must learn to access that consortium of wisdom.

Ideas to Contemplate:

1. Accessing this wisdom requires being able to focus your intent and manage the movement of your energy.

2. This wisdom is accessed through vertical consciousness.

3. In which areas of your life do you find your energy moving horizontally? What result does this movement create? What is manifested?

4. In which areas of your life do you move your energy vertically? What is manifested through this movement?

5. Goodness, integrity, and wisdom are gifts from God. They affect who you are, how you see yourself, and how you define yourself in the world. How have they influenced your life?

Week 40

Reflection:

The true key to loving others is recognizing that sharing abundance is part of your growth toward self-realization. Truly, giving to others is giving to yourself, and loving others is not possible unless you love yourself. A sense of abundance, of more than enough for all, resides in a grateful heart.

Ideas to Contemplate:

1. Self-realization is the movement toward freedom and living consciously. Self-realization does not come from taking on more rules or another person's truth—it comes from removing the veils of ignorance that have prevented you from seeing your own truth and your own magnificence and beauty.

2. Where in your life do you sense and experience abundance?

3. How can you share this abundance with others?

4. What did you receive in sharing your abundance?

Week 47

Reflection:

*We must know and embrace all of what we are. Whatever we choose **not** to look at will end up ruling our lives.*

Ideas to Contemplate:

1. Are you jealous of the beauty in others? How do you feel about your own beauty?

2. How do you relate to someone else's success?

3. Is there an emotional chasm within yourself that is unsatisfied?

4. What resonates in you when you meet your most successful, beautiful friend? Is it support or envy?

5. Ask yourself, "Who creates the obstacles in my life?"

A Circle of Completion—Part I

Reflection:

You sit in the center of your own circle of truth, in ever-increasing stillness, knowing that you have indeed accomplished what you have come onto this earth to do. You have made your mark. You have added to the world in some way. You have manifested your truth and your beauty, and now a kind of stillness inhabits you. You begin to watch life in all its mystery, like a great wise one who is full of love and power.

Sacred Practice—Completion:

It is time to take stock of what you have accomplished this year. The challenge is to do this without judgment, to stand in the place of the sacred witness and be totally honest as you look into the mirror of your own life, to see all that you have done and all that you have left undone. To be honest about yourself without judgment is the ultimate act of self-love and an important step on your path to self-realization. For the next four weeks, I want you to use the wheel for this Sacred Practice and write about these questions in your Personal Pages.

SOUTH—How have you brought love into your physical existence? How are you loving your body? What is your home environment like?

WEST—How have you brought love into the west, the place of emotions? How are you emotionally expressing love?

NORTH—How do you experience love in your spiritual life? Describe your experiential relationship to God or the Great Spirit.

EAST—How have you brought love into your mental realm? Do you love the way your mind works?

Week 49

A Circle of Completion—Part II

Reflection:

Open your heart to contain all of who you are, all of what life truly is; this is the path of mastery.

Sacred Practice—Completion:

Continue taking stock of what you have accomplished this year. The challenge remains doing this without judgment, standing in the place of the sacred witness and being totally honest as you look into the mirror of your own life, seeing all that you have done and all that you have left undone. Being honest about yourself without judgment is the ultimate act of self-love and an important step on your path to self-realization. For the next three weeks, I want you to continue using the wheel for this Sacred Practice, and write about these questions in your Personal Pages.

SOUTH—How have you brought power into your physical world? Are you comfortable expressing power through your body? Do you feel powerful in your environment?

WEST—How have you brought power into your emotional vocabulary? Are you comfortable expressing power through your emotions? Do you feel powerful in your emotions?

NORTH—How have you brought power into your spiritual experience? Are you comfortable expressing power as a spiritual attribute?

EAST—How have you brought power into the world of your mind? Are you comfortable expressing power through your words and thoughts?

Week 50

A Circle of Completion—Part III

Reflection:

In mastery you become aware of a different kind of light. That light is a reflection of the flaws of your being, as if a rainbow prism of light were reflecting off a crack in a crystal. It is within the flaws of your being that mastery is found.

Sacred Practice—Completion:

Continue taking stock of what you have accomplished this year. The challenge remains doing this without judgment, standing in the place of the sacred witness and being totally honest as you look into the mirror of your own life, seeing all that you have done and all that you have left undone. Being honest about yourself without judgment is the ultimate act of self-love and an important step on your path to self-realization. Continue using the wheel for this Sacred Practice, and write about these questions in your Personal Pages.

SOUTH—How are you manifesting love and power in your environment?

WEST—What has transformed in your relationship to love and power?

NORTH—How has balancing love and power in your life moved you closer to spiritual mastery?

EAST—How has balancing love and power changed the way you think about yourself in the world?

A Circle of Completion—Part IV

Reflection:

Once the gateways to all possibilities have opened, your life will be filled with extraordinary shifts and changes. Listen well and love well; the answers to your questions are all around you.

Sacred Practice—Completion:

It is time to complete this four-week circle of taking stock of your accomplishments for the year. The challenge remains doing this without judgment, standing in the place of the sacred witness and being totally honest as you look into the mirror of your own life, seeing all that you have done and all that you have left undone. Being honest about yourself without judgment is the ultimate act of self-love and an important step on your path to self-realization. Again, use the wheel for this Sacred Practice, and write about these questions in your Personal Pages.

SOUTH—Do you have a place in your home to bring in Spirit—a meditation area, a small altar, or a place where you consciously honor your acts of vertical movement and communication?

WEST—How do you bring together your emotions and your mind?

NORTH—How have you brought spirit into your day-to-day life?

EAST—Do you feel balanced in bringing your emotions into the realm of your mind?

CENTER—How has this year of self-discovery changed your point of view?

Week 52
A Circle of Gratitude

Reflection:

When you meet the challenge of exploring your own depths, you will be rewarded with even more light. Be grateful for the magnificent life you have been graced with, grateful for the experience of the forces of nature that surround you, grateful for the consciousness and the awareness to experience Spirit in your life. It is in this state of grace, living within the heartbeat of God and the Goddess, that you experience a life of mastery and bliss.

Sacred Practice—Gratitude:

It is time to celebrate what you have accomplished this year! What you have left **undone** is as much a part of your accomplishment as what you have **done**. Celebrate it all, and find a place within yourself where these two opposites become one. Look at this past year from the place of the sacred witness. Are you judging yourself for not doing this work perfectly? Is there some issue or obstacle that seems to be standing in the way of you and your evolvement toward self-realization? Remember, it is within the flaws of your being that mastery is found, just as it is in the flaw of a crystal that we find the rainbow gateway.

Sit for a moment. Simply sit in silent reflection honoring and acknowledging all of the experiences and all of the people in your life that fill you with gratitude. Living in the presence of grace, you can discover a way to remove or release the obstacles in your path. Focusing on gratitude, you will feel yourself expand, able to contain even more love and power. Who in your life are you truly grateful for? Let them know. Thank them for their gifts. Express your gratitude to them. And always, always express your gratitude to yourself. Do something very special for yourself. You deserve it!

Remember, as you complete one turn of the wheel, another begins. We are always moving. It has been my honor and my joy to have shared this work with you. I send you my love and my blessings as you continue your journey around the sacred wheel of life.

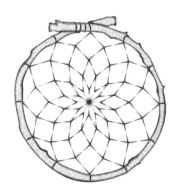

Personal Pages

Personal Pages

Personal Pages

Personal Pages

Personal Pages

Personal Pages

Personal Pages

Personal Pages

Personal Pages

Personal Pages

Personal Pages

Personal Pages

Personal Pages

Personal Pages

Personal Pages

Personal Pages

Personal Pages

Personal Pages

Personal Pages

Personal Pages

Personal Pages

Personal Pages

Personal Pages

Personal Pages

Personal Pages

Personal Pages

Personal Pages

Personal Pages

Personal Pages

Personal Pages

Personal Pages

Personal Pages

Personal Pages

Personal Pages

Personal Pages

Personal Pages

Personal Pages

Personal Pages

Personal Pages

Personal Pages

Personal Pages

Personal Pages

Personal Pages

Personal Pages

Personal Pages

Personal Pages

Personal Pages

Personal Pages

Personal Pages

Personal Pages

Personal Pages

Personal Pages

Personal Pages

Personal Pages

Personal Pages

Personal Pages

Personal Pages

Personal Pages

Personal Pages

Personal Pages

Personal Pages

Personal Pages

Personal Pages

Personal Pages

Personal Pages

Personal Pages

Personal Pages

Personal Pages

Personal Pages

Personal Pages

Personal Pages

Personal Pages

Personal Pages

Personal Pages

Personal Pages

Personal Pages

Personal Pages

Personal Pages

Personal Pages

Personal Pages

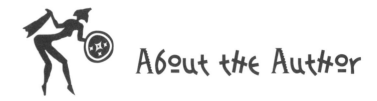

About the Author

Lynn V. Andrews is the internationally acclaimed author of 16 books, including *The Medicine Woman Series* and *The Power Deck;* and she is currently published in 12 languages. Considered an inspirational teacher in the field of personal development, Lynn is a 20th-century shaman whose work continually leads us into a powerful exploration of self-discovery and spirituality.

Enter a Cosmology of Mystery, Magic, and Power with Lynn Andrews . . .

"For over ten years, I have been describing my learning and my path. It has been a joy to do this. In continuing my journey, I would be grateful if you would share your insights with me.

"You are also invited to join me at my annual spring retreat for four days of ceremony, sacred community, meditation, and healing. In addition, expanded in-depth training is available through the Lynn Andrews Center for Sacred Arts and Training, a home study course beginning each February. Please call or write for schedule dates and detailed information. Also available are over 20 audiocassettes, beautifully produced and digitally recorded, including guided meditations and a very special selection of teachings, personal reflections, and sacred music."

— Lynn Andrews

Please send Lynn your name and address
so she can share any new information with you:

Lynn Andrews
2934 ½ Beverly Glen Circle
Box 378
Los Angeles, CA 90077
(800) 726-0082

Website: **www.lynnandrews.com**

Other Hay House Titles of Related Interest

EMPOWERING WOMEN, by Louise L. Hay

A GARDEN OF THOUGHTS: My Affirmation Journal, by Louise L. Hay

A JOURNAL OF LOVE AND HEALING, by Sylvia Browne and Nancy Dufresne

THE LIGHTWORKER'S WAY, by Doreen Virtue, Ph.D.

THOUGHTS OF POWER AND LOVE, by Susan Jeffers, Ph.D.

7 PATHS TO GOD, by Joan Borysenko, Ph.D.

VISIONSEEKER, by Hank Wesselman, Ph.D.

THE WORKBOOK OF SELF-MASTERY, by John Randolph Price

We hope you enjoyed this Hay House Lifestyles book.
If you would like to receive a free catalog featuring
additional Hay House books and products,
or if you would like information about the
Hay Foundation, please contact:

Hay House, Inc.
P.O. Box 5100
Carlsbad, CA 92018-5100

(760) 431-7695 or **(800) 654-5126**
(760) 431-6948 (fax) or **(800) 650-5115 (fax)**

Please visit the Hay House Website at: **www.hayhouse.com**